Level F • Book 2

QuickReads®
A Research-Based Fluency Program

Elfrieda H. Hiebert, Ph.D.

MODERN CURRICULUM PRESS

Pearson Learning Group

Program Reviewers and Consultants

Dr. Barbara A. Baird
Director of Federal Programs/Richardson ISD
Richardson, TX

Dr. Kate Kinsella
Dept. of Secondary Education and Step to College Program
San Francisco State University
San Francisco, CA

Pat Sears
Early Child Coordinator/Virginia Beach Public Schools
Virginia Beach, VA

Dr. Judith B. Smith
Supervisor of ESOL and World and Classical Languages/Baltimore City Public Schools
Baltimore, MD

The following people have contributed to the development of this program:

Art and Design: Kathleen Ellison, Denise Ingrassia, Salita Mehta,
    Dan Thomas, Dan Trush

Editorial: Lynn W. Kloss

Marketing: Alison Bruno

Production/Manufacturing: Louis Campos, Michele Uhl

Publishing Operations: Jennifer Van Der Heide

Modern
Curriculum
Press

Pearson Learning Group

1-800-321-3106
www.pearsonlearning.com

Contents

Contents

Contents

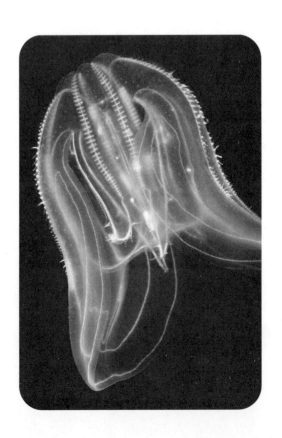

SCIENCE **The Changing Earth**

Contents

Acknowledgments

All photography © Pearson Education Inc. (PEI) unless otherwise specifically noted.

Cover: Kim Heacox/Getty Images, Inc. 3: Jorg & Petra Wegner/Animals Animals/Earth Scenes. 4: David Woodfall/Peter Arnold, Inc. 5: AP/Wide World Photo. 6: Gregory G. Dimijian/Photo Researchers, Inc. 7: © Roger Ressmeyer/Corbis. 8: Martin Harvey/Peter Arnold, Inc. 10: Getty Images, Inc. 12: Jorg & Petra Wegner/Animals Animals/Earth Scenes. 14: SuperStock, Inc. 16: SuperStock, Inc. 18: © Raymond Gehman/ Corbis. 24: David Woodfall/Peter Arnold, Inc. 26: *l.* Peter Anderson/ DK Images; *r.* Lawrence Migdale Photography. 28: © Gabe Palmer/ Corbis. 30: Rudi Von Briel/PhotoEdit. 32: AP/Wide World Photo. 38: AP/Wide World Photo. 40: AP/Wide World Photo. 42: Otto Stadler/Das Fotoarchiv/Peter Arnold, Inc. 44: Michael Newman/ PhotoEdit. 46: Dana White/PhotoEdit. 54: Viola's photos/Animals Animals/Earth Scenes. 56: Gregory G. Dimijian/Photo Researchers, Inc. 58: Roland Birke/Peter Arnold, Inc. 60: Y. Gladu/Photo Researchers, Inc. 66: © Roger Ressmeyer/Corbis. 68: OAR/National Undersea Research Program (NURP); Univ. of Hawaii/NOAA Photo Library. 70: © Dean Conger/ Corbis. 72: © Bryn Colton/Corbis. 74: *l.* © 2001 Gary Braasch; *r.* © 2001 Gary Braasch/World View of Global Warming. 80: Mark Edwards/ Peter Arnold, Inc. 82: *t.* © Ed Romano/Corbis; *b.* © Corbis. 84: AP/Wide World Photo. 88: Martin Harvey/Peter Arnold, Inc.

Wetlands

Wetlands are home to a large number of plants and animals.

What Are Wetlands?

Although all climates have wetlands, wetlands are quite different from one another. Wetlands are found in both desert and arctic climates. The[25] water in wetlands can be either salt water from the ocean or fresh water from rivers, lakes, or rain. Wetlands can also last all year[50] or only one season.

What is the same about wetlands is their water level. The water in wetlands is at or near the surface of[75] the land. In addition, wetlands are usually less than six feet deep.

The main kinds of wetlands are marshes, swamps, and bogs. Marshes have grasses[100] and plants with soft stems. Swamps have trees and shrubs. Bogs are covered with peat. Peat is made up of dead plants that have already[125] decayed or have begun to decay. The plants in a peat bog grow very densely in the wet ground.[144]

Wetlands

Birds, like these storks, find safe places to live and feed in wetlands.

Wetlands and Earth

Wetlands are important to the cycle of life on Earth. Many birds and fish live in wetlands all or part of the[25] time. Many plants also grow in wetlands, feeding on the rich soil. As plants die, bacteria break them down into nutrients. Then, this nutrient-rich[50] water helps other plants to grow.

During rainy seasons, the soil in wetlands absorbs water from rivers. By absorbing river water, wetlands help prevent flooding[75] that could destroy homes and crops. In addition, the stored water is useful in dry seasons, when it is absorbed by the roots of plants.[100]

Wetlands can also remove some dangerous pollutants from water. Sediment, which is tiny grains of matter that are heavier than water, settles to the bottom[125] of wetlands. Pollutants in this sediment often do less harm in wetlands than in topsoil or water.[142]

Wetlands

The Everglades, in Florida, is protected as a national park.

Wetlands in the United States

The Everglades, in southern Florida, has more than 900 kinds of plants and 600 kinds of animals in its marshes,[25] swamps, dry islands, and open water. The number of insect species that live there is even higher.

Before the importance of wetlands was recognized, parts[50] of the Everglades were drained, and canals and pumps changed the flow of the water. Today, though, a large part of the Everglades is protected[75] as a national park and cannot be drained.

The wetlands in the plains and deserts of the Southwest look quite different from the Everglades wetlands.[100] In the Southwest, wetlands are usually dry for long periods. However, even during dry periods, Southwestern wetlands may have water just below the surface of[125] the land. As they do in the Everglades, many animals raise their young in these Southwestern wetlands.[142]

Wetlands

Windmills have been used for hundreds of years in the Netherlands to pump water from the land.

A Nation Built on Wetlands

The Netherlands is a country in northern Europe that is located where three rivers flow into the North Sea. When[25] the Romans conquered this area more than 2,000 years ago, it was mostly wetlands. The Romans created dry land by building canals to drain the[50] water away. Until recently, the people of the Netherlands continued to drain wetlands.

Half of the Netherlands is below sea level. Pumps and a system[75] of canals keep it dry. For many years, the pumps were powered by windmills. Today, electricity powers the pumps.

Much of the land in the[100] Netherlands that was once wetlands is now used for homes and businesses. However, the people of the Netherlands recognize the importance of wetlands. In the[125] past 30 years, they have restored some wetlands, allowing them to fill with water once again.[141]

Wetlands

The ponds in many golf courses both challenge
golfers and allow birds to rest and feed.

Saving Wetlands

As people recognize the importance of wetlands, they are working to restore and maintain them. Arcata, California, for example, uses wetlands, not chemicals,[25] to treat its wastewater. The plants and bacteria in Arcata's wetlands break down the pollutants in its wastewater.

The Central Valley of California was once[50] filled with wetlands. These wetlands were used by many bird species as they traveled between their winter and summer homes. Then, people decided to grow[75] rice in the wetlands. Today, birds and people share part of the Central Valley's wetlands. Birds use them to rest and feed, and people use[100] them to grow rice.

In the southeastern United States, some golf courses are restoring wetlands. Golf courses often use water to challenge golfers. By adding[125] a wetland to a golf course, people support the environment and challenge golfers at the same time.[142]

Write words that will help you remember what you learned.

What Are Wetlands?

_____

_____

_____

_____

Wetlands and Earth

_____

_____

_____

_____

Wetlands in the United States

_____

_____

_____

_____

A Nation Built on Wetlands

_____

_____

_____

_____

Saving Wetlands

_____

_____

_____

_____

What Are Wetlands?

1. How are wetlands alike?

   Ⓐ Peat, swamps, and bogs grow in them.

   Ⓑ They contain salt water and fresh water.

   Ⓒ Their water level is the same during all seasons.

   Ⓓ They have water at or near the surface of the land.

2. Name two ways wetlands are different from one another.

   _____

   _____

   _____

Wetlands and Earth

1. Another good name for "Wetlands and Earth" is ___

   Ⓐ "Why We Need Wetlands."

   Ⓑ "Pollutants and Wetlands."

   Ⓒ "The Life Cycle of Wetlands."

   Ⓓ "Wetlands in the Rainy Season."

2. How can wetlands remove pollutants from water?

   _____

   _____

   _____

Wetlands in the United States

1. "Wetlands in the United States" is MAINLY about ___

   (A) how wetlands formed in the United States.

   (B) important U.S. wetlands.

   (C) how people use wetlands in the United States.

   (D) how U.S. wetlands were destroyed.

2. How are the Southwestern wetlands different from the Everglades wetlands?

   _____

   _____

   _____

A Nation Built on Wetlands

1. How do the people of the Netherlands keep their land dry?

   (A) by draining the rivers

   (B) with pumps and canals

   (C) by building homes on the land

   (D) with electricity

2. How did the Romans change the land in the Netherlands?

   _____

   _____

   _____

Saving Wetlands

1. "Saving Wetlands" is MAINLY about ___

   Ⓐ why plants and animals depend on wetlands.

   Ⓑ how people restore and maintain wetlands.

   Ⓒ the wetlands of Arcata, California.

   Ⓓ golf courses that are built on wetlands.

2. How are people learning to live with wetlands?

   _____

   _____

   _____

Connect Your Ideas

1. How has the way people treat wetlands changed over the years?

   _____

   _____

   _____

2. What are three ways that wetlands help people and animals?

   _____

   _____

   _____

Managing Garbage

Countries around the world are looking for ways to manage the large amounts of garbage their people create every day.

The Problem of Garbage

Garbage is material that people no longer want. For hundreds of years, people threw their garbage onto the street, where it^{25} often caused disease.

As the number of people increases, the amount of garbage increases, too. More people buy, and throw away, more goods. This means^{50} that more and more garbage must be managed.

Most countries in North America and Europe have sewage systems that clean dirty water and other liquids.^{75} Solid waste, however, can be difficult to manage because it takes up a lot of space. In addition, it can be toxic, or poisonous, to^{100} plants and animals.

Solid waste consists of material such as food scraps, grass clippings, clothes, and paper towels. Toxic waste consists of material such as^{125} paint and batteries. Around the world, governments are working to find ways to solve the problem of garbage.^{143}

Managing Garbage

Some solid waste can be recycled, like the vegetables in this garden and the cans that were used to make this artwork.

Decreasing Garbage

In 2001, the United States created about 230 million tons of solid waste. This means that every American created about 4.4 pounds of [25] garbage every day.

The best solution to the garbage problem is to decrease the amount of it. Many groups are showing people how to reduce, [50] reuse, and recycle garbage. Recharging batteries reduces both garbage and toxic waste.

Today, Americans recycle about 30 percent of their garbage. However, experts say that [75] much more garbage can be recycled. Americans recycle only five of every ten cans. Nearly 40 percent of all garbage is made up of paper [100] and cardboard. Often, grass clippings and food scraps are also thrown into the garbage. However, if this material is allowed to decay, it makes the [125] soil richer. Both recycling and reducing waste can decrease the amount of garbage countries must manage. [141]

Managing Garbage

Toxic waste in landfills can be dangerous to the people,
animals, and soil nearby.

Landfills

Most garbage that is not recycled goes into landfills. State and national governments have rules about landfills. Rules describe the barriers needed to keep [25] toxic waste from leaking into the soil and water. Rules also tell how much dirt must cover the layers of garbage and what to do [50] with landfill gases. When landfills are full, they are sealed. However, experts continue gathering information on the air, water, and soil nearby.

Some towns have [75] made sealed landfills safe, then used the land to build golf courses and parks. One such park in Virginia, called Mount Trashmore, became a park [100] after many years of work. Mount Trashmore even has skateboard pits.

Today, the United States has about 3,000 active landfills. Few new landfills are being [125] built. This is because of the cost and because few people want to live or work near landfills. [143]

Managing Garbage

Garbage in the ocean can harm large and small marine animals.

Garbage and the Oceans

Garbage can make the oceans unsafe for people, animals, and plants. Some countries believe that oceans are big enough to handle[25] garbage, so they dump it off their shores. Other ocean garbage comes from liquids that run off the land. More than 600 million gallons of[50] oil ends up in oceans each year. Much of this oil comes from people cleaning out their cars and trucks.

Toxic waste in oceans also[75] comes from factories, farms, and home-cleaning materials. This toxic waste settles into the sediment on the ocean floor. Tiny sea animals then feed on[100] the sediment, taking in toxic waste with their food. Tiny sea animals also eat bits of decayed plastic that look like food. Once such toxic[125] waste gets into the food chain, it harms bigger and bigger animals. Finally, it harms humans.[141]

Managing Garbage

Large numbers of computer discs are starting to appear in landfills.

Garbage and the Future

Governments and communities continue to create ways to manage garbage. Even as more garbage is recycled, though, new garbage problems arise.[25]

Often, new inventions create garbage problems. The invention of cars, for example, helped people travel great distances. However, car tires must be replaced, and tires[50] do not decompose in landfills. Today, there are mounds of tires in landfills, and the mounds keep growing.

The invention of computers has also changed[75] people's lives. Like tires, computers do not decompose. Already, millions of computers are piled in landfills around the world. These computers contain toxic metals that[100] can poison the water and soil.

Every day, governments and communities look for new ways to manage garbage. Their greatest needs are to find ways[125] to reduce the amount of garbage people create and to keep garbage from harming life on Earth.[142]

Managing Garbage

Write words that will help you remember what you learned.

The Problem of Garbage

_____

_____

_____

_____

Decreasing Garbage

_____

_____

_____

_____

Landfills

_____

_____

_____

_____

Garbage and the Oceans

_____

_____

_____

_____

Garbage and the Future

_____

_____

_____

_____

The Problem of Garbage

1. What is garbage?

   Ⓐ liquid waste

   Ⓑ material that is toxic to animals

   Ⓒ solid waste

   Ⓓ material that people no longer want

2. Why is solid waste difficult to manage?

   _____

   _____

   _____

Decreasing Garbage

1. "Decreasing Garbage" is MAINLY about ___

   Ⓐ how to reduce the amount of garbage.

   Ⓑ why garbage is toxic to people and animals.

   Ⓒ how to find new places to dump garbage.

   Ⓓ which kinds of paper can be recycled.

2. What are two ways to decrease garbage?

   _____

   _____

   _____

Managing Garbage

Landfills

1. What are landfills?

   Ⓐ places where recycled materials are kept

   Ⓑ places where solid waste is reused

   Ⓒ places where garbage is dumped

   Ⓓ places that are made into golf courses and parks

2. What are two kinds of rules governments have made about landfills?

   _____

   _____

   _____

Garbage and the Oceans

1. Another good name for "Garbage and the Oceans" is ___

   Ⓐ "Cleaning Up the Oceans."

   Ⓑ "Getting Rid of Toxic Waste."

   Ⓒ "The Problem of Ocean Garbage."

   Ⓓ "Ocean Animals and Garbage."

2. How can toxic waste in the oceans harm humans?

   _____

   _____

   _____

Garbage and the Future

1. Why are people looking for new ways to manage garbage?

   Ⓐ so computers do not become toxic waste

   Ⓑ to keep it from harming life on Earth

   Ⓒ so people will recycle their garbage

   Ⓓ to keep all of Earth's garbage together

2. Describe how a new invention created a garbage problem.

   _____

   _____

   _____

Connect Your Ideas

1. How has the treatment of garbage changed from long ago to now?

   _____

   _____

   _____

2. Why is managing garbage a problem today?

   _____

   _____

   _____

Purchasing Power

Money can be used to buy goods or services.

The Value of Money

A 100-dollar bill and a one-dollar bill have the same kind of paper and ink. The paper used in[25] both bills also has the same value, and the two bills cost the same amount to print. However, 100-dollar bills and one-dollar bills[50] have different values. More work is required to earn a 100-dollar bill than a one-dollar bill. A 100-dollar bill can also buy[75] more than a one-dollar bill.

The word *currency* describes the paper money and coins that are "current" in a country. Before the 1930s, a[100] country needed to have an amount of gold that equaled the amount of currency it circulated. Gold is no longer needed to back up the[125] currency that countries circulate. However, if a country circulates too much currency, other countries may value it less.[143]

Purchasing Power

How much you can buy in another country depends on
that country's exchange rate.

Dollars, Pesos, and Yen

Each country's government controls the value of the money it circulates. In the United States, the unit of money is the[25] dollar. Mexico uses the peso, while Japan uses the yen.

Airplanes and computers make it easy for people to visit and do business around the[50] world. That means that people must exchange their money for the money of the country they visit or work with.

Today, each country's money is[75] valued against the money of other countries. The value of one country's currency compared to the value of another country's currency is called the exchange[100] rate. The exchange rate is the amount of money a person receives for exchanging one currency for another currency. Exchange rates change from day to[125] day. In the first part of 2005, one U.S. dollar was worth 11 pesos or 104 yen.[142]

Purchasing Power

Euros are now used in most countries in the European Union.

A Common Currency

The countries in Europe, such as Germany, France, and Italy, are close together. However, until 2002, all three countries used different currencies.[25] Travelers exchanged German marks for French francs, or French francs for Italian lira.

In 2002, Germany, France, Italy, and nine other European countries began to[50] use the same currency. This new currency was called the euro. Euro banknotes in all 12 European Union countries look the same. Euro coins, though,[75] look the same on only one side. Each country uses its own design on the other side. German marks, French francs, and Italian lira are[100] no longer used.

The single currency has made it easier to travel and do business in the European Union. As of 2005, only three countries[125] in the European Union did not use the euro. Instead, they used their own currency.[140]

Purchasing Power

Credit cards let people purchase goods without using cash.

Credit Cards

Credit cards were introduced in the United States in 1950. Cash machines were not available, so travelers purchased goods with cash or credit[25] cards.

Today, many people purchase goods with credit cards. People apply to banks or similar institutions to get a credit card. If the application is[50] accepted, the person and the institution sign a legal agreement. This agreement lists the rules for using the credit card.

Typically, the institution pays for[75] the goods or services the person purchases. Then, the person pays the institution back. The institution charges interest, or extra money, for bills the person[100] does not pay right away. Usually, the person pays the institution a fee for using the credit card.

Credit cards can be convenient, but they[125] can also be costly. The interest on unpaid bills can make things cost much more than their original price.[144]

Purchasing Power

The cost of digital video discs has gone down as the supply has gone up.

Supply and Demand

The cost of products is influenced by two ideas: supply and demand. The way in which supply and demand works can be [25] seen with the cost of machines that play digital video discs, or DVD players.

In 1997, when DVD players first appeared in stores, they cost [50] almost $1,000. The demand for DVD players was low because their price was high. Usually, when an item's price is high, the demand for it [75] is low.

Supply also determines price. When the demand for DVD players was low, few factories made them. As DVD players became more popular, though, [100] more factories began making them. Companies saw that they could make money by making DVD players, so the supply grew. By 2005, people could purchase [125] DVD players for as little as $50. When the supply becomes greater than the demand, prices go down. [143]

Purchasing Power

Write words that will help you remember what you learned.

The Value of Money

_____

_____

_____

_____

Dollars, Pesos, and Yen

_____

_____

_____

_____

A Common Currency

_____

_____

_____

_____

Credit Cards

_____

_____

_____

_____

Supply and Demand

_____

_____

_____

_____

The Value of Money

1. "The Value of Money" is MAINLY about ___

   Ⓐ how much money is circulated in other countries.

   Ⓑ why all countries use the same currency.

   Ⓒ how much money is worth.

   Ⓓ why people use money.

2. What is currency?

_____

_____

_____

Dollars, Pesos, and Yen

1. People need to exchange their money in other countries because ___

   Ⓐ different countries use different currencies.

   Ⓑ other countries do not use currency.

   Ⓒ pesos can only be used in Japan.

   Ⓓ their money only has value at home.

2. What is the exchange rate?

_____

_____

_____

A Common Currency

1. What is the euro?

   Ⓐ a currency used in the European Union

   Ⓑ the exchange rate in Europe

   Ⓒ the currency that replaced the dollar

   Ⓓ the name of the European Union

2. How does the euro help people travel and do business in the European Union?

   _____

   _____

   _____

Credit Cards

1. How can credit cards make goods cost more?

   Ⓐ They help buyers spend more money.

   Ⓑ They charge interest on unpaid bills.

   Ⓒ They give buyers extra money to spend.

   Ⓓ They tell banks what people purchase.

2. How do credit cards work?

   _____

   _____

   _____

Supply and Demand

1. The main idea of "Supply and Demand" is that ___

   Ⓐ supply and demand are the same thing.

   Ⓑ buyers decide how much to pay for things.

   Ⓒ both supply and demand determine prices.

   Ⓓ many companies make goods when prices are high.

2. What are supply and demand?

   _____

   _____

   _____

Connect Your Ideas

1. What are three facts you learned about money in this topic?

   _____

   _____

   _____

2. Suppose there was another reading in this topic. Do you think it would be about banks or about traveling in Europe? Why?

   _____

   _____

   _____

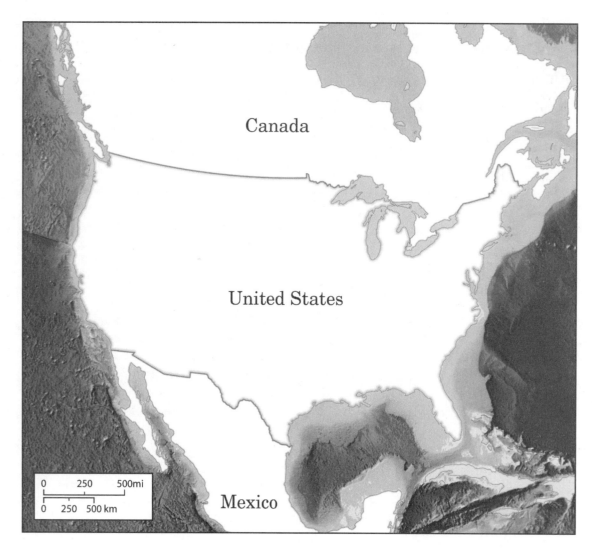

On this map, the lighter areas in the oceans around Canada, the
United States, and Mexico show the continental shelves.

The World Beneath the Ocean's Surface

Because oceans cover about 70 percent of Earth, most of Earth's land is under water. People have sailed the [25] ocean for several thousand years. However, most of what is known about the world below the ocean's surface was discovered in the last century. Compared [50] to Earth's surface, which people have explored for thousands of years, the world beneath the ocean's surface is largely unexplored.

Every continent is surrounded by [75] a kind of shelf, called a continental shelf. The water in the continental shelves is only a few hundred feet deep. Beyond this area, the [100] ocean floor slopes down sharply. Like dry land, the ocean floor has plains, mountain ranges, and valleys. The ocean's average depth is 12,200 feet, or [125] about 2.3 miles, but its deepest point is more than 36,000 feet, or about 6.8 miles, beneath the surface. [144]

Beneath the Ocean's Surface

The world in the first layer of the ocean is rich in plant and animal life.

Ocean Layers

People who study the ocean divide it into five layers, or zones. Like climate zones on land, each ocean layer offers different living [25] conditions for plants and animals. The first layer is thinnest. This layer extends to about 660 feet below the ocean's surface. Sunlight penetrates the first [50] layer of ocean and supports the growth of many kinds of plants and animals.

As the water grows deeper, less and less light penetrates the [75] darkness. The second layer, which extends from about 660 feet to about 3,300 feet, is a sort of twilight zone. Little light extends to this [100] depth, and the water pressure increases. The bottom three layers are even deeper and colder, and the pressure increases greatly. Relatively little is known about [125] the deepest layers of the ocean because they are hard for people to explore safely. [140]

Beneath the Ocean's Surface

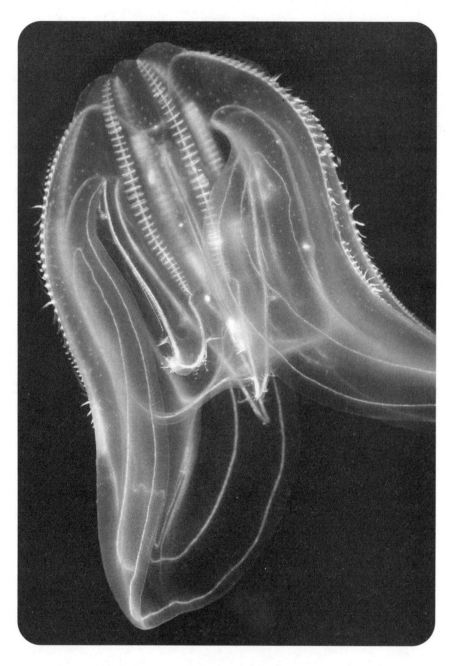

This jellyfish has adapted to the darkness of the ocean by producing its own light.

Light and Ocean Life

Marine animals that live in the deepest layers of the ocean have developed ways to move around and find food. Some[25] animals have adapted to the darkness by producing their own light. Parts of their bodies emit light, which they use to lure food, attract mates,[50] or blind enemies.

Some marine animals have adapted by spending time both near the surface and in the deep layers of the ocean. Because sperm[75] whales breathe air, they must come to the surface often. Near the surface, they use their eyes to navigate. However, when sperm whales travel to[100] the deep ocean for food, they navigate with sound. Sperm whales emit sounds, then they detect the sounds' echoes as they are reflected by objects[125] in the water. These echoes help sperm whales "see" in the darkness of the deep ocean.[141]

Beneath the Ocean's Surface

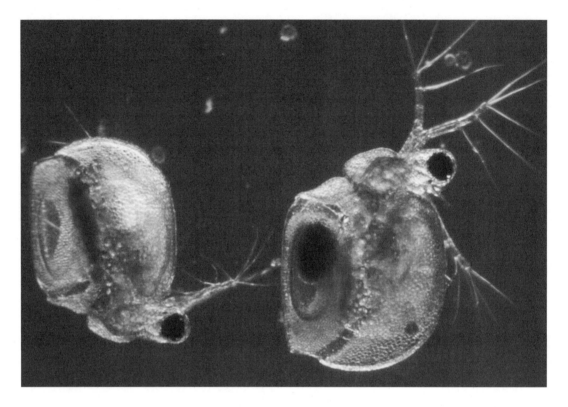

Zooplankton, like these water fleas, live in the ocean in huge numbers.

The Ocean's Food Chain

Unlike animals, plants can produce their own food. As a result, life on land and in the ocean depends on plants.[25] Plants produce food, and animals consume it.

The ocean's food chain begins with tiny plants called phytoplankton. Phytoplankton float at, or near, the surface. Tiny[50] sea animals called zooplankton consume phytoplankton. Zooplankton, in turn, are eaten by small fish, shrimps, and clams. Larger fish, such as tuna and sharks, then[75] eat these animals. Finally, killer whales eat tuna and sharks. This sequence is often called a food chain.

Many food chains in the ocean depend[100] on one another. In zones where plants can't grow, animals eat the dead bodies and waste products of animals that live in higher zones. The[125] food chains of the ocean form a complex food web that begins with tiny phytoplankton and zooplankton.[142]

Beneath the Ocean's Surface

Underwater vessels help people explore the deepest parts of the ocean.

Exploring the Ocean

Diving suits and oxygen tanks allow people to explore the surface layer of the ocean. However, people face two problems when they[25] explore the deep ocean. They must carry oxygen so that they can breathe, and they must protect themselves from the water pressure. Because of these[50] problems, only about 2 to 5 percent of the ocean has been explored.

Early explorations used machines called dredges. Dredges, which were lowered from ships,[75] brought back material from the ocean floor. In the 1920s, sound waves provided the first accurate information about the ocean's depth.

Today, underwater vessels travel[100] in the deep ocean. People on ships guide these underwater vessels with remote controls. Only one manned vessel has gone to the deepest part of[125] the ocean. In 1960, this manned vessel stayed on the ocean floor for only 20 minutes.[141]

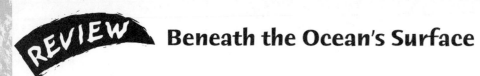

Beneath the Ocean's Surface

Write words that will help you remember what you learned.

The World Beneath the Ocean's Surface

_____

_____

_____

_____

Ocean Layers

_____

_____

_____

_____

Light and Ocean Life

_____

_____

_____

_____

The Ocean's Food Chain

_____

_____

_____

_____

Exploring the Ocean

_____

_____

_____

_____

The World Beneath the Ocean's Surface

1. The ocean floor is ___

   (A) deepest near the continents.

   (B) the same depth around the world.

   (C) flat beyond the continental shelves.

   (D) deepest beyond the continental shelves.

2. Describe the land beneath the ocean's surface.

   _____

   _____

   _____

Ocean Layers

1. "Ocean Layers" is MAINLY about ___

   (A) how the ocean changes as it gets deeper.

   (B) how sunlight reaches the bottom of the ocean.

   (C) the animals that live on the ocean floor.

   (D) the water pressure on the ocean floor.

2. Explain how the light and water pressure change in the ocean's layers.

   _____

   _____

   _____

Beneath the Ocean's Surface

Light and Ocean Life

1. The main idea of this reading is ___

   Ⓐ how light travels in the ocean.

   Ⓑ marine animals that emit their own light.

   Ⓒ how sperm whales breathe and find food in the ocean.

   Ⓓ how marine animals adapted to darkness in the ocean.

2. How do sperm whales navigate both near the surface and deep in the ocean?

   _____

   _____

   _____

The Ocean's Food Chain

1. A food chain is ___

   Ⓐ phytoplankton and zooplankton.

   Ⓑ animals that eat phytoplankton.

   Ⓒ how animals and plants make and eat food.

   Ⓓ the plants that grow in the ocean.

2. Describe an ocean food chain.

   _____

   _____

   _____

Exploring the Ocean

1. Which of the following help people explore the surface layer of the ocean?

   Ⓐ diving suits and oxygen tanks

   Ⓑ underwater vessels and diving suits

   Ⓒ phytoplankton and oxygen tanks

   Ⓓ oxygen tanks and dredges

2. What are two ways people have explored the deep layers of the ocean?

   _____

   _____

   _____

Connect Your Ideas

1. Tell three facts you learned about the ocean in this topic.

   _____

   _____

   _____

2. Describe the deep ocean, and tell how people explore it.

   _____

   _____

   _____

Earthquakes can make large changes in Earth's surface.

Changes in Earth's Surface

Although Earth's surface seems to stay the same, in fact, it is constantly changing. It is easy to see large-scale,[25] sudden changes to Earth's surface, such as volcanic eruptions and earthquakes. However, events such as volcanic eruptions and earthquakes are only part of the changes[50] to Earth's surface that occur every day.

Every day, the Rocky Mountains grow a little higher. The Appalachian Mountains wear down. Soil from rivers and[75] streams adds land to the coastlines of rivers and oceans. Rocks and chunks of soil that were part of coastlines fall into rivers and oceans.[100]

Individual people do not live long enough to see changes that happen to Earth's surface slowly, such as the shifting of continents or the wearing[125] down of mountain ranges, like the Appalachians. However, Earth's surface does change in small stages every day.[142]

The Changing Earth

The robot at the top of the picture is checking the temperature
of the lava on Lo'ihi.

A New Hawaiian Island

The state of Hawaii has eight major islands and many small islands. The islands were formed over millions of years by [25] underwater volcanoes in the Pacific Ocean. Lava poured out of these underwater volcanoes and hardened on the volcanoes' cones. When a cone rose above the [50] ocean's surface, a new Hawaiian Island was visible.

Today, many underwater volcanoes are active. In fact, a name has already been given to an island [75] that scientists predict will one day become a new Hawaiian Island. Its name is Lo'ihi, which means "long" in the Hawaiian language.

Currently, Lo'ihi rises [100] about 3,000 feet from the ocean floor, but it is still under water. In another 10,000 to 100,000 years, Lo'ihi will probably have produced enough [125] lava to lift the volcano's cone above the ocean's surface. When that happens, Hawaii will have a new island. [144]

The Changing Earth

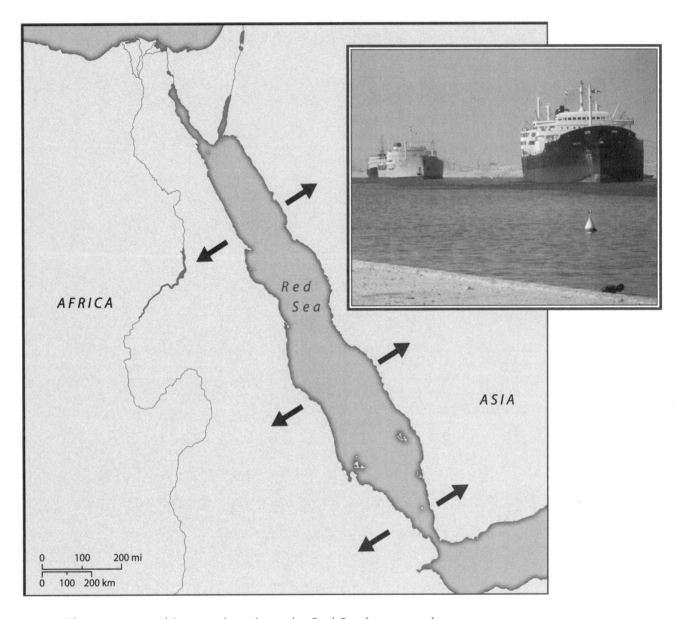

The arrows on this map show how the Red Sea has moved over many years. The picture shows large ships on the Red Sea today.

Inch by Inch

The Red Sea lies between the continents of Asia and Africa. Scientists believe that the two continents were once connected. However, over[25] millions of years, Africa pulled away from Asia. This movement resulted in deep rifts, or rips, in Earth's surface.

As the continents pulled apart, water[50] from nearby oceans and seas seeped into the rifts. Over millions of years, the area of water grew large enough to be called a sea.[75] Because the sea turns red when large numbers of a kind of tiny sea creature dies, it is called the Red Sea.

The movement in[100] Earth's surface that created the Red Sea is still happening. Scientists report that Africa moves about a half-inch away from Asia each year. At[125] this rate, in about 100 years, Africa may be about four feet farther from Asia than it is today.[144]

Shoreline erosion caused this house to fall into the sea.

Shoreline Erosion

The shorelines of oceans are constantly changing. Usually, the changes are gradual. In parts of central California, the heavy waves of winter storms [25] erode, or wear away, about four inches of shoreline each year. The results of this gradual erosion can be seen in pictures of the same [50] place that were taken at different times.

In the early 1900s, Natural Bridges got its name because rocks formed three arches at the edge of [75] the shoreline. Today, two of the three arches are gone. Scientists predict that the third arch will erode, too.

Sometimes, however, a shoreline changes suddenly. [100] This happened in December 2004, when huge waves raced onto the shores of several countries around the Indian Ocean. More than 150,000 people were killed [125] by the waves. In addition, large parts of beaches, cliffs, and headlands were washed away. [140]

The Changing Earth

The picture on the left shows the Rhone glacier in 1859.
The picture on the right was taken in the same place in 2001.

Glaciers

Today, about 160,000 glaciers, or masses of ice, cover about 10 percent of Earth's land. The rate at which glaciers advance and retreat depends[25] on Earth's climate. At the peak of the last Ice Age, glaciers covered about 32 percent of Earth. As the glaciers advanced, they dug large[50] valleys in Earth's surface. Later, when the glaciers retreated, water filled the valleys and formed lakes. The Great Lakes of North America were formed in[75] this way.

Although glaciers advance and retreat very slowly, photographs and paintings can show how glaciers change. In 1859, an artist painted a picture of[100] the Rhone glacier in Europe. At that time, the glacier filled an entire valley of the Alps Mountains. Today, so much of the Rhone glacier[125] has melted that a person sitting in the same spot would only see a small bit of it.[143]

The Changing Earth

Write words that will help you remember what you learned.

Changes in Earth's Surface

_____

_____

_____

_____

A New Hawaiian Island

_____

_____

_____

_____

Inch by Inch

_____

_____

_____

_____

Shoreline Erosion

_____

_____

_____

_____

Glaciers

_____

_____

_____

_____

Changes in Earth's Surface

1. The main idea of this reading is that ___

   Ⓐ Earth's surface changes a few times each year.

   Ⓑ mountains do not change on Earth's surface.

   Ⓒ Earth's surface changes constantly.

   Ⓓ the land on the continents stays the same.

2. What are two ways Earth's surface changes?

   _____

   _____

   _____

A New Hawaiian Island

1. What is Lo'ihi today?

   Ⓐ one of Hawaii's major islands

   Ⓑ an underwater volcano in Hawaii

   Ⓒ a scientist who named a Hawaiian volcano

   Ⓓ a kind of underwater lava

2. How were the Hawaiian Islands formed?

   _____

   _____

   _____

The Changing Earth

Inch by Inch

1. Another good name for "Inch by Inch" is ___

   Ⓐ "Forming the Red Sea."

   Ⓑ "Connected Continents."

   Ⓒ "Asia and Africa."

   Ⓓ "Earth's Surface."

2. How was the Red Sea formed?

   _____

   _____

   _____

Shoreline Erosion

1. What is shoreline erosion?

   Ⓐ a winter storm that damages the shore

   Ⓑ the wearing away of a coastline

   Ⓒ a shoreline in California

   Ⓓ damage from huge waves

2. What are two ways shorelines can be changed?

   _____

   _____

   _____

Glaciers

1. Which of the following affects the advance and retreat of glaciers?

   Ⓐ how valleys and lakes are created

   Ⓑ the amount of land that is covered by ice

   Ⓒ Earth's climate

   Ⓓ the movement of Earth

2. Describe how glaciers formed the Great Lakes of North America.

_____

_____

_____

Connect Your Ideas

1. Describe two ways in which Earth's surface changes slowly.

_____

_____

_____

2. Describe two ways in which Earth's surface changes quickly.

_____

_____

_____

Environmental Disasters

This photograph shows land in Haiti that was once covered with trees.

What Is an Environmental Disaster?

When an environmental disaster occurs, large numbers of plants and animals, and even Earth itself, are damaged. Sometimes, one event [25] causes the damage, such as a ship spilling oil into the ocean. At other times, the damage is caused by activities that happen over many [50] years.

Currently, Haiti is suffering from environmental damage caused by years of forest clearing. In 1950, about two of every five square miles of Haiti [75] were covered with forest. Since then, people have cut millions of trees to make farmland and firewood. Today, only about one of every 100 square [100] miles of Haiti is covered with forest.

Clearing so much forest has led to many environmental problems. With few trees to hold the soil in [125] place, heavy rains create floods that kill people and wash away the topsoil needed to grow food. [142]

Environmental Disasters

Some people in the Pennsylvania valley wore masks to protect themselves from the smog.

Killer Smog

On Tuesday, October 26, 1948, heavy fog settled into a narrow river valley in Pennsylvania. For years, people in the valley had noticed[25] smoke from a factory that smelted, or separated, metal from ore. On this day, though, the fog held the smoke near the ground. Because no[50] fresh air could get in to blow it away, the fog and smoke formed a thick smog.

The smog stayed in the Pennsylvania valley for[75] almost a week. During this time, although many people had trouble breathing, the smelting factory kept producing smoke.

Finally, on Sunday, the smelting factory was[100] shut down, and rain arrived and began to break up the smog. By that time, however, 7,000 people had become sick and 20 people had[125] died. This environmental disaster led to the first state and federal laws to control the quality of air.[143]

Environmental Disasters

This child was poisoned in the Minamata disaster.

Deadly Substances

In the 1940s, people in the seaside town of Minamata, Japan, noticed that cats and other animals were acting strangely. Some cats seemed to dance into the sea, where they drowned. By the 1950s, some people in the town were also acting strangely. By 1956, many people were very ill and others had died. Finally, it was found that a local company had been spilling mercury compounds into the bay near the town for more than 20 years.

The people and animals of Minamata had eaten fish from the bay for many years. Then, scientists found that the fish had deposits of mercury compounds in their bodies. As people and animals ate the fish, deposits of mercury compounds built up inside them. The Minamata disaster showed how deadly substances can get into the food chain and harm many species.

Environmental Disasters

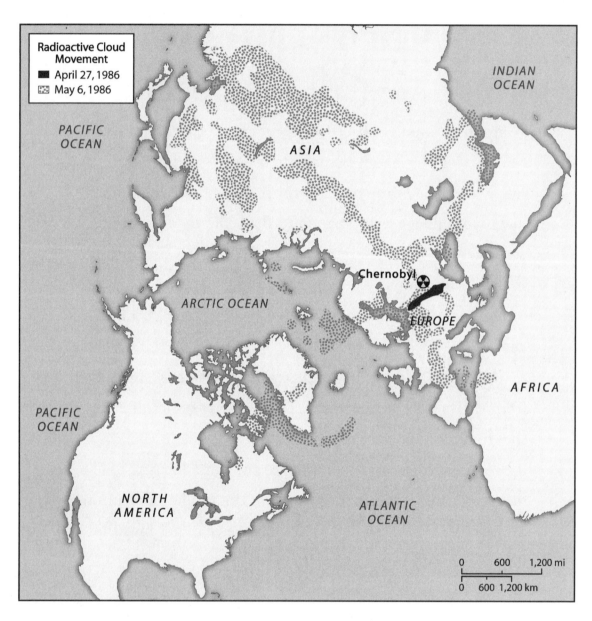

Radioactive Cloud Movement
April 27, 1986
May 6, 1986

PACIFIC OCEAN

INDIAN OCEAN

ASIA

ARCTIC OCEAN

Chernobyl

EUROPE

AFRICA

PACIFIC OCEAN

NORTH AMERICA

ATLANTIC OCEAN

0   600   1,200 mi

0   600 1,200 km

This map shows how the radiation from Chernobyl spread
around the world.

Nuclear Accidents

Nuclear power plants can provide large amounts of cheap energy. However, accidents at nuclear power plants are costly to people, animals, and the [25] environment. A nuclear explosion throws radiation into the air that affects all living things. Radiation in the soil affects plants for years. Radioactive particles in [50] the air or in food can also cause serious health problems for people and animals.

In 1986, the world's largest nuclear accident happened near Chernobyl, [75] a small city in Ukraine. Several large explosions at the nuclear power plant were followed by fires. Almost nine tons of radioactive material escaped into [100] the air and the soil. More than 100,000 people were moved from Chernobyl to other parts of Ukraine. And, although hundreds of thousands of workers [125] tried for several years to clean up the radioactive material, many people became ill from the high radiation levels. [144]

Environmental Disasters

Many marine animals, like this penguin, can be seriously hurt
or killed by oil spills.

Black Tide

Although there are many kinds of environmental disasters, oil spills are particularly harmful to plants and animals. On November 13, 2002, an oil[25] tanker named the *Prestige* sank off the coast of Spain. The ship broke in two, spilling more than 60,000 tons of oil into the ocean.[50]

Oil came ashore in black tides, covering rocks and beaches for miles. Marine animals and birds could not breathe or stay warm because oil matted[75] their fur or feathers. Large numbers of plants, fish, birds, and other animals died.

Although oil is extremely difficult to remove, an expensive clean-up[100] effort was begun. The shore was washed one rock at a time. Years later, most of the oil had been recovered. The beaches look clean.[125] However, scientists continue to find oil in the sand, where it can still harm plants and animals.[142]

Environmental Disasters

Write words that will help you remember what you learned.

What Is an Environmental Disaster?

_____

_____

_____

_____

Killer Smog

_____

_____

_____

_____

Deadly Substances

_____

_____

_____

_____

Nuclear Accidents

_____

_____

_____

_____

Black Tide

_____

_____

_____

_____

What Is an Environmental Disaster?

1. Which of the following BEST describes an environmental disaster?

   Ⓐ damage to farmlands and forests

   Ⓑ living things that damage one another

   Ⓒ forest clearings that damage a species

   Ⓓ damage to large numbers of plants and animals

2. What is causing environmental damage in Haiti?

   _____

   _____

   _____

Killer Smog

1. Smog is ___

   Ⓐ any environmental disaster.

   Ⓑ a mixture of fog and rain.

   Ⓒ smoke from factories.

   Ⓓ a mixture of fog and smoke.

2. How did people try to prevent killer smog from happening again?

   _____

   _____

   _____

Environmental Disasters

Deadly Substances

1. What caused the environmental disaster in Minamata?

   Ⓐ fish and cats that were ill

   Ⓑ mercury spilled into a bay

   Ⓒ the people of Minamata

   Ⓓ the food chain

2. Describe the environmental disaster in Minamata.

   _____

   _____

   _____

Nuclear Accidents

1. "Nuclear Accidents" is MAINLY about ___

   Ⓐ the risks of air pollution.

   Ⓑ the effects of radiation.

   Ⓒ why nuclear power plants explode.

   Ⓓ nuclear power plants in Ukraine.

2. What happened in the Chernobyl accident?

   _____

   _____

   _____

Black Tide

1. What is a black tide?

    Ⓐ a ship that spills oil and water

    Ⓑ a way to clean coastlines

    Ⓒ oil that is spilled into water

    Ⓓ animals that are hurt by oil spills

2. Why are black tides called environmental disasters?

    _____

    _____

    _____

Connect Your Ideas

1. Describe how two kinds of environmental disasters can harm people,
   animals, and plants.

    _____

    _____

    _____

2. What are two things that could be done to keep environmental disasters
   from happening?

    _____

    _____

    _____

Reading Log • Level F • Book 2

	I Read This	New Words I Learned	New Facts I Learned	What Else I Want to Learn About This Subject
Wetlands				
What Are Wetlands?				
Wetlands and Earth				
Wetlands in the United States				
A Nation Built on Wetlands				
Saving Wetlands				
Managing Garbage				
The Problem of Garbage				
Decreasing Garbage				
Landfills				
Garbage and the Oceans				
Garbage and the Future				
Purchasing Power				
The Value of Money				
Dollars, Pesos, and Yen				
A Common Currency				
Credit Cards				
Supply and Demand				

	I Read This	New Words I Learned	New Facts I Learned	What Else I Want to Learn About This Subject
Beneath the Ocean's Surface				
The World Beneath the Ocean's Surface				
Ocean Layers				
Light and Ocean Life				
The Ocean's Food Chain				
Exploring the Ocean				
The Changing Earth				
Changes in Earth's Surface				
A New Hawaiian Island				
Inch by Inch				
Shoreline Erosion				
Glaciers				
Environmental Disasters				
What Is an Environmental Disaster?				
Killer Smog				
Deadly Substances				
Nuclear Accidents				
Black Tide				

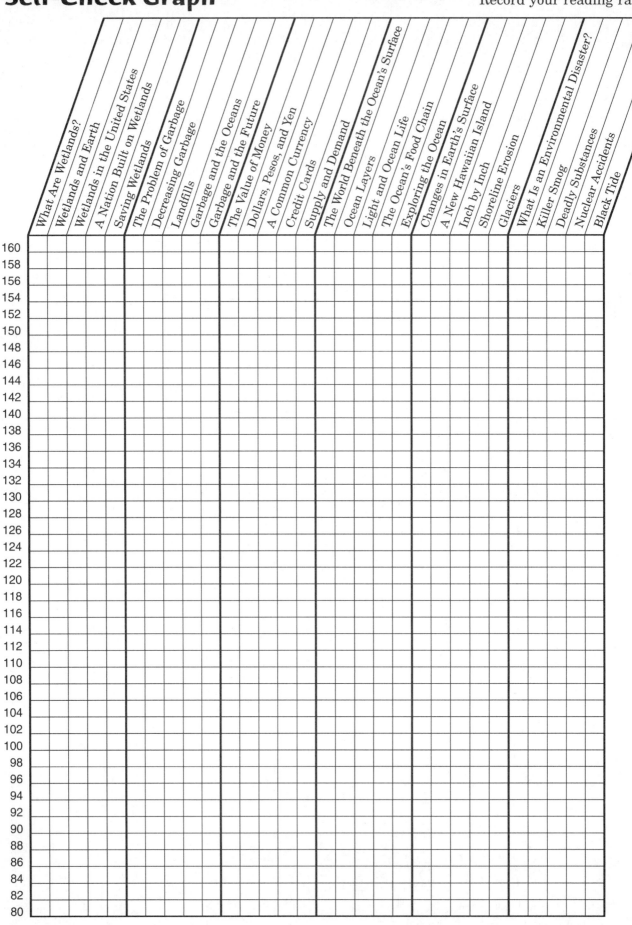

Column headers (left to right): What Are Wetlands? · Wetlands and Earth · Wetlands in the United States · A Nation Built on Wetlands · Saving Wetlands · The Problem of Garbage · Decreasing Garbage · Landfills · Garbage and the Oceans · Garbage and the Future · The Value of Money · Dollars, Pesos, and Yen · A Common Currency · Credit Cards · Supply and Demand · The World Beneath the Ocean's Surface · Ocean Layers · Light and Ocean Life · The Ocean's Food Chain · Exploring the Ocean · Changes in Earth's Surface · A New Hawaiian Island · Inch by Inch · Shoreline Erosion · Glaciers · What Is an Environmental Disaster? · Killer Smog · Deadly Substances · Nuclear Accidents · Black Tide

Vertical axis values: 160, 158, 156, 154, 152, 150, 148, 146, 144, 142, 140, 138, 136, 134, 132, 130, 128, 126, 124, 122, 120, 118, 116, 114, 112, 110, 108, 106, 104, 102, 100, 98, 96, 94, 92, 90, 88, 86, 84, 82, 80